ART MASTERCLASS WITH WASSILY KANDINSKY

WIDE EYED EDITIONS

Brimming with creative inspiration, how-to projects, and useful information to enrich your everyday life, Quarto Knows is a favourite destination for those pursuing their interests and passions. Visit our site and dig deeper with our books into your area of interest: Quarto Creates, Quarto Cooks, Quarto Homes, Quarto Lives, Quarto Drives, Quarto Explores, Quarto Gifts, or Quarto Kids.

Art Masterclass with Kandinsky © 2018 Quarto Publishing plc. Text © 2018 Quarto Publishing plc. Illustrations © 2018 Quarto Publishing plc.

First published in 2018 by Wide Eyed Editions, an imprint of The Quarto Group. The Old Brewery, 6 Blundell Street, London N7 9BH, United Kingdom. T (0)20 7700 6700 F (0)20 7700 8066 www.QuartoKnows.com

The right of Hanna Konola to be identified as the illustrator of this work has been asserted by her in accordance with the Copyright, Designs and Patents Act, 1988 (United Kingdom).

All rights reserved.

No part of this publication may be reproduced, stored in a retrieval system, or transmitted, in any form, or by any means, electrical, mechanical, photocopying, recording or otherwise without the prior written permission of the publisher or a licence permitting restricted copying.

A catalogue record for this book is available from the British Library.

ISBN 978-1-78603-170-9
The illustrations were created digitally
Set in Gotham Rounded

Published by Jenny Broom and Rachel Williams
Designed by Nicola Price
Edited by Katie Cotton
Production by Kate O'Riordan

Manufactured in Shenzhen, China HH 022018

1 3 5 7 9 8 6 4 2

MAKE ART LIKE KANDINSKY!

In this masterclass, you'll learn how to draw and paint like one of the most important artists of the twentieth century, Wassily Kandinsky. But first, you'll need to make sure you have a few things ready:

PAINTS
Kandinsky used all different kinds of paints to achieve the effect he wanted, including:

PENCILS
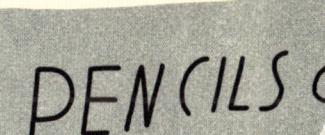
Get lots, some sharp and some not so sharp!

WATERCOLOUR
This is a delicate paint that you mix with water. The more water you use, the more washed out the colour will be.

OIL
Because it has oil in it, this paint is much thicker than watercolour.

COLOURING PENCILS, CRAYONS AND FELT TIPS
Have as many colours as you can.

GOUACHE
This is also mixed with water, usually before it's put in tubes. But unlike watercolour, gouache doesn't show the paper through it.

TEMPERA

Colour pigment is mixed with something else, normally egg yolk, to make tempera. It dries very quickly.

A MIXTURE

It's possible that Kandinsky used different types of paint on the same artwork, so don't be afraid to mix it up!

BRUSHES

Different brushes will do different things, so it's good to have a range, like round, flat, pointed, big and small.

Whether you use pencils or paints, you can still learn how to make art like Kandinsky!

MEET THE MASTER

Wassily Kandinsky was born on December 4, 1866, in Moscow, Russia.

From a young age, he loved colour – in fact, as a child, when he was given his first paint box from an aunt, he said he heard the different colours making a hissing sound. Some people think he had a condition called synaesthesia, which allows people to hear colours or see sounds.

Kandinsky studied law and economics and lectured at the University of Moscow before deciding to study art at age 30. He is considered to be one of the most important artists of the twentieth century, and many people think he created the first 'abstract' painting.

Abstract means a painting without any recognisable images in it, like people or a landscape. Instead of trying to copy reality, Kandinsky used colours and shapes to say something, or to respond to a piece of music. Towards the end of his life, Kandinsky went further, focusing on rigid geometric shapes like triangles and circles in his paintings.

He died in 1944, but his influence on art is still felt today.

1866 — Wassily Kandinsky is born on December 4, 1866, in Moscow

1886 — Kandinsky begins to study law and economics at the University of Moscow, but experiences 'unusual' feelings about colour!

1896 — Changing his life forever, Kandinsky moves to Munich, Germany to study art, first at a private school and then at the Munich Academy.

1903 — Kandinsky has his first one-man show in Moscow, followed by two others in Poland the year after.

1906 — During a two-year journey across Europe, Kandinsky discovers Impressionism and develops his own style, which becomes more and more abstract.

1910 — Kandinsky creates First Abstract Watercolour, considered by some to be the first abstract painting.

1911 — Kandinsky co-founds Der Blaue Reiter (The Blue Rider) – a group of like-minded artists that seek to express spiritual truths in art.

1912 — *Concerning the Spiritual in Art* is published by Kandinsky, in which he argues that the artist has a responsibility to the 'inner voice' of art, rather than to the trends of the day or their own personality.

1914 — World War One breaks out. Kandinsky returns to Russia where, over the next few years, he creates the Institute of Artistic Culture and becomes director of the Moscow Museum for Pictorial Culture.

1922 — Kandinsky accepts a teaching post in the famous Bauhaus school of architecture and applied art in Weimar.

1933 — The Nazis force the Bauhaus to close. Kandinsky moves to France, where he lives for the rest of his life. 57 of Kandinsky's paintings are confiscated by the Nazis in the 1937 purge of 'degenerate art'.

1944 — Kandinsky dies on December 13, in Neuilly-sur-Seine.

1. HOW TO SEE LIKE KANDINSKY

Do you think a painting should look like something in real life? Kandinsky didn't! Even when he was inspired by things that happened in reality, he never really copied at all. This made him different from many other artists of the time. Kandinsky is called an 'abstract' artist. This means that the things in his art were simplified or changed so that they no longer looked like they did in real life.

Look at this picture Kandinsky painted in 1911.

Can you see any people or animals in this picture?

What else can you see?

Does the picture look different if you turn it the other way up? Which do you think is the best way of looking at the picture?

Copy Kandinsky's picture on the next page, and write a title in the label at the bottom. What do you think the painting is of? Do you want to add anything else to it?

When you've copied the picture and written its title, read the answer below to see what Kandinsky was actually painting.

[upside-down text:] Kandinsky called this painting 'Impression V (Park)'. The correct way up is how it is in the book. If you look closely, you can see two people in yellow, sitting on a bench, and a tree in the top right corner.

2. HOW TO MAKE ABSTRACT ART LIKE KANDINSKY

It doesn't matter whether you thought the painting on the previous page was a park or not. Kandinsky thought the colours and shapes in a picture were more important than the viewer being able to recognise what was in it. Create your own abstract picture by following these steps!

Draw a picture in this box of something you like. It could be a picture of a park, a beach, your house or school. In this picture, you should copy how it is in real life, using the same colours as you can see when you look at it.

Now, draw the picture again in this box, but this time, make it abstract! Instead of copying the scene exactly, use rough shapes or lines. For example, rather than drawing a person, you can just use a straight line, or a circle. Instead of drawing a house with a chimney and a front door, you can just draw a square. And instead of using the 'right' colours, use different ones.

How different do the paintings look? Which one do you like best?

3. HOW TO DRAW AN IMPROVISATION LIKE KANDINSKY

Kandinsky sometimes created 'impressions' of the world around him, like the one of the park in the first lesson. However, he often preferred to draw from his imagination or be inspired by a feeling - drawing spontaneous pictures that he called 'improvisations'. For example, he created this one, called Improvisation 9, in 1910.

This picture wasn't something that Kandinsky saw happening. Instead, it was a scene that he imagined.

Can you see any person in this picture? What are they doing?

Where do you think the rider is going?

What are the shapes in the bottom left of the picture?

In the white box, draw your own improvisation based on a castle. What is happening in the castle? Who lives there? Is someone special visiting? Remember, you don't have to make everything look like real life. Instead, you can use shapes and different colours, just like Kandinsky.

MY IMPROVISATiON
((ASTLE)

4. HOW TO COLOUR LIKE KANDINSKY

Kandinsky was fascinated by colour from a very young age. He didn't think colours were only important because of how they looked. Kandinsky thought colours could feel a certain way, or be hot and cold, or even have different sounds. Most of all, they could change how the reader felt. He said, 'Colour is a power which directly influences the soul.'

Get some pencils and paints and choose which colours are:

- SMOOTH
- STICKY
- SOFT
- WARM
- HARD
- COLD

Now think about how colours might make you think of different sounds, and how sounds might make you think of different colours. Look at this picture by Kandinsky called Composition no. 4:

What do you think the different colours below would sound like? Do you agree with Kandinsky?

YELLOW

Kandinsky thought this colour sounded high-pitched like a mouse.

I think yellow sounds like...

RED

Kandinsky thought this colour sounded strong like a trumpet.

I think red sounds like...

DARK BLUE

Kandinsky thought this colour sounded low like a cello.

I think blue sounds like...

GREEN

Kandinsky thought this colour sounded like a quiet violin.

I think green sounds like...

----

5. COLOUR IN THESE KANDINSKY PAINTINGS

Now practise your colouring in with this painting, copying the colours Kandinsky used. Why do you think he chose these shades? What do you think the painting is about?

Why do you think Kandinsky put a red dot in this picture?

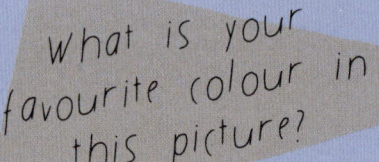

What is your favourite colour in this picture?

Kandinsky drew these circles as an experiment to see how different combinations of colours would look.

Try painting or colouring your own circles in the grid below.

Which one do you think looks best?

6. HOW TO LISTEN LIKE KANDINSKY

Music was very important to Kandinsky. In 1911, he went to an Arnold Schoenberg concert, which sounded different to other music of the time. Most people thought it was strange, but not Kandinsky. He wrote to Schoenberg saying, 'You have realised in your work that which I... have so long sought from music.' He created a painting of the concert, called Impression III (Konzert), to show the effect the music had on him.

Can you see the people listening to the music?

Can you spot a big black shape that looks like a piano?

Some people think the yellow is the music itself, wrapping around the people. What do you think the music was like?

Listen to a piece of music. It can be
anything you like – classical or pop, old
or modern. If you prefer, you can watch
an artist performing, just like Kandinsky.
Write down the name of the artist and
the piece of music here.

- -

Now draw a picture of how the music makes you feel.
Use different colours for the different sounds.
If you like, you can draw people listening to the music,
like in Kandinsky's picture.

7. HOW TO DRAW A HORSE AND RIDER LIKE KANDINSKY

Kandinsky painted lots of things throughout his lifetime, but there was one thing he kept coming back to in his pictures. He liked to draw a horse with a rider on it. For Kandinsky, this had a special meaning. The horse-and-rider symbolised art, and they were on a journey to make the world a better place.

Look at these different pictures, each with a horse and rider in it. Where do you think each of the riders are going on their horses? Make up a short story for the one you like best.

This rider is going to the castle because...

This rider has a spear because...

This rider is travelling...

My Horse and Rider Story

Draw your own picture of a horse and rider here.

My Horse and Rider Picture

8. HOW TO DRAW CIRCLES LIKE KANDINSKY

As his life went on, Kandinsky used more and more shapes in his work. He believed that paintings didn't have to copy something in real life, or show a place or people. Colours and shapes were fine on their own. Circles were possibly Kandinsky's favourite shape. He thought they were perfectly balanced, and could even make the person looking at the painting have spiritual thoughts.

Before you make pictures like Kandinsky, practise drawing circles here. You might find it harder than it looks!

Now think about why circles are important. Can you think of anything in real life that looks like a circle? What about the sun, or a watch, or a ring? Draw on these circles to make them different objects.

This is one of Kandinsky's most famous paintings using circles. Try copying it in the space below.

If you want, you can add even more circles than Kandinsky did.

9. HOW TO USE SHAPES LIKE KANDINSKY

Kandinsky also liked to use other shapes, like triangles and squares. He thought circles made the viewer think spiritual thoughts, whereas he thought triangles were angry shapes and squares were calm.

Practise drawing these different shapes in the spaces on this page. Can you think of things these shapes look like?

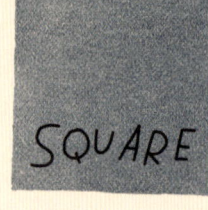
KITE

----

looks like a kite.

TRIANGLE

CRESCENT

SQUARE

----

looks like a triangle.

----

looks like a crescent.

----

looks like a square.

SEMI-CIRCLE

RECTANGLE

----

looks like a semi-circle.

----

looks like a rectangle.

Now look at this painting by Kandinsky.

What is your favourite colour in this painting?

Do the triangles on the right remind you of anything?

The painting is called Weiches Hart, which means 'Soft Hard'. Which of the shapes are hard and which do you think are soft?

Using some soft shapes and some hard shapes, plus any other shapes you like, draw your own picture in the box below.

MY SHAPES PICTURE

10. COMPLETE THE KANDINSKY PICTURE USING STICKERS

Where each shape went in the artwork was important to Kandinsky, as he thought it affected how the person looking at the picture felt. But the painting on the opposite page has some missing shapes!

Can you find the stickers at the back of the book to finish it off? You don't have to put the pieces exactly where Kandinsky put them. Try experimenting by putting them in different places and seeing how the picture changes. Which combination do you like best?

11. DRAW YOUR OWN KANDINSKY EXHIBITION

Congratulations! You've learnt how to draw and colour like Kandinsky, from creating art from your imagination to using shapes in your pictures. Now you're ready to practise more by drawing your own Kandinsky-inspired art collection! All these people have come to visit the gallery. What are they going to see?

Shapes

Impression I

12. CREATE A COMPOSITION LIKE KANDINSKY

The biggest paintings Kandinsky drew were called compositions. This was the third of his types of paintings. Impressions were paintings based on the world around him, like the one of the park in lesson 1.

Improvisations were spontaneous pictures, drawn from his imagination or inspired by a feeling. But compositions were different. Kandinsky considered them to be his most complicated and important paintings, and only drew ten of them during his lifetime.

This picture is called Composition VII, and it was painted in 1913.

Kandinsky didn't tell his reader what the picture was of, but we know from his writings that one of his themes was Deluge (meaning flood). Do any of the colours and shapes in this picture make you think of a flood? If not, what do they make you think of?

Five steps to create your own composition:

1 To create your own composition like Kandinsky, first choose a theme. What do you want to create an artwork about? It could be a flood (as in Kandinsky's painting), or a zoo, or someone's first day at school, or Christmas, or something else altogether!

Write down what your painting will be about here:

What words does your theme make you think of? Write them down here:

2 Next, think about what colours you want to use, and play with them here in this box. Do you want to use colours that are hard, squeaky, sticky, warm or something else?

3 Now, think about what shapes you'd like to use, and draw them here. Are you using hard shapes, or soft shapes, or a mixture of both? If there will be animals or people or buildings in your painting, what shapes will you give them?

4 Explore your ideas by sketching! Kandinsky created over 30 drawings and paintings for Composition VII before he started on the final artwork. You don't have to do that many, but you should try and do a few.

Composition Study 1

Composition Study 2

Composition Study 3

Composition Study 4

When you're ready, create your composition on the pull-out poster in the back of the book. Take the best bits from your work on this page, but feel free to add new things if you like. You can use pencils, paints, stickers and whatever else you like to explore your theme. Just enjoy it!

image credits

Where there are multiple images on a page, the pictures are credited top to bottom.

Page 4: **Vassily Kandinsky, c.1906**; © SZ Photo / Sammlung Megele / Bridgeman Images

Page 6: **Impression V (Park), 1911;** Kandinsky, Wassily (1866-1944) / Musee National d'Art Moderne, Centre Pompidou, Paris, France / De Agostini Picture Library / M. Carrieri / Bridgeman Images

Page 10: **Improvisation 9, 1910 (oil on canvas);** Kandinsky, Wassily (1866-1944) / Private Collection / Bridgeman Images

Page 13: **Composition no. 4, 1911 (oil on canvas);** Kandinsky, Wassily (1866-1944) / Kuntsammlung Nordrhein-Westfalen, Dusseldorf, Germany / Peter Willi / Bridgeman Images

Page 14: **Laison, 1932 (oil on canvas);** Kandinsky, Wassily (1866-1944) / Private Collection / Photo © Christie's Images / Bridgeman Images

Page 15: **Concentric Circles, 1913 (oil on canvas);** Kandinsky, Wassily (1866-1944) / Private Collection / Bridgeman Images

Page 16: **Impression no. 3 (Concert) 1911 (oil on canvas);** Kandinsky, Wassily (1866-1944) / Stadtische Galerie im Lenbachhaus, Munich, Germany / Bridgeman Images:

Page 18:
Improvisation III, 1909 (oil on canvas); Kandinsky, Wassily (1866-1944) / Musee National d'Art Moderne, Centre Pompidou, Paris, France / Peter Willi / Bridgeman Images
St. George, 1914-15 (oil on cardboard); Kandinsky, Wassily (1866-1944) / Tretyakov Gallery, Moscow, Russia / Bridgeman Images
Lyrical, 1911; Kandinsky, Wassily (1866-1944) / Museum Boymans van Beuningen, Rotterdam, The Netherlands / Bridgeman Images

Page 21: **Sketch for Several Circles, 1926 (oil on paper laid on canvas);** Kandinsky, Wassily (1866-1944) / NOMA New Orleans Museum OF Art, USA / Bridgeman Images

Page 23: **Weiches Hart (Soft Hard) 1927 (oil on canvas);** Kandinsky, Wassily (1866-1944) / Galerie Maeght, Paris, France / Peter Willi / Bridgeman Images

Page 24: **Composition Number 8, 1923 (oil on canvas);** Kandinsky, Wassily (1866-1944) / Solomon R. Guggenheim Museum, New York, USA / Bridgeman Images

Page 28: **Composition No. 7, 1913 (oil on canvas),** Kandinsky, Wassily (1866-1944) / Tretyakov Gallery, Moscow, Russia / Bridgeman Images